# FLOWERS

## in Medieval Manuscripts

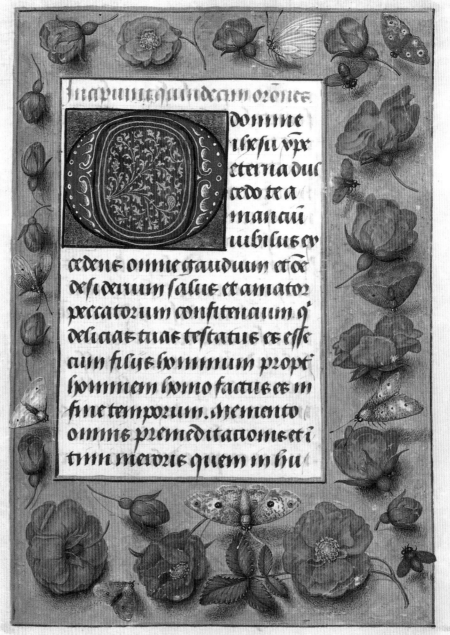

Incipiunt quindecim oratones

O domine
ihesu xpe
eterna dul
cedo te a
manaū
iubiluset ex
cedens omne gaudium et oē
desiderium salus et amator
peccatorum confitentatum q̄
delicias tuas testatus es esse
cum filijs hominum propt
hominem homo factus es in
fine temporum. memento
omnis premeditationis et i
tum meroris quem in hu

# FLOWERS
## in Medieval Manuscripts

CELIA FISHER

UNIVERSITY OF TORONTO PRESS

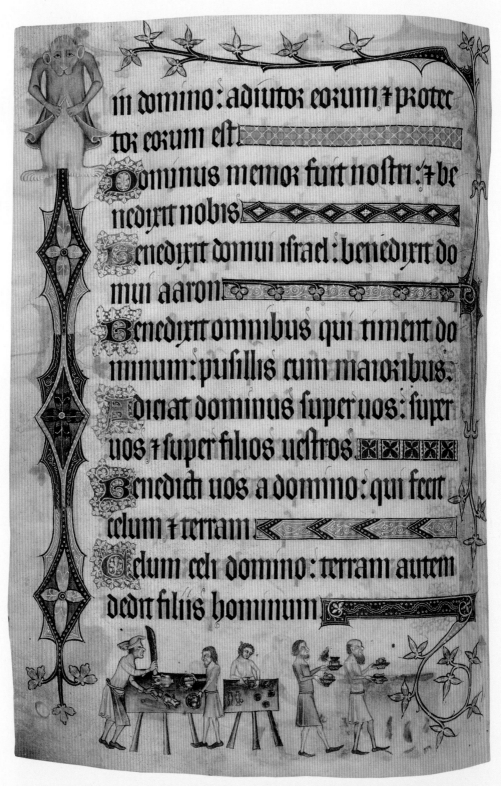

in domino: adiutoz eozum ꝓ protec
toz eozum est

Dominus memoz fuit nostri: ꝰ be
nedizit nobis

Benedizit domui israel: benedizit do
mui aaron

Benedizit omnibus qui timent do
minum: pusillis cum maioribus.

Adiciat dominus super uos: super
uos ꝰ super filios uestros

Benedicti uos a domino: qui fecit
celum ꝰ terram

Celum celi domino: terram autem
dedit filiis hominum

1. Border and initial decorations which include trefoils, ivy, oak and vine leaves from the Luttrell Psalter. English, c.1300. Add. MS 42130, f.207v.

# THE SIGNIFICANCE OF PLANTS

Plants appear in art for two principal reasons: because they are decorative or because they mean something. These two reasons are not mutually exclusive. On the contrary, successive artists who have depicted plants in their work have balanced aesthetics with deliberate symbolism, or given a more unconscious evocation of the spirit of their times. There is also a third dimension, realism: in order to read the message contained in an artistic depiction of a plant it is necessary to recognise the plant.

Although flower decoration in illuminated manuscripts reached its peak in the fifteenth century, the origins of flower decoration lie much earlier. For within the medieval period it became customary for the large decorative capital letters marking the beginnings of chapters or prayers to be decorated with tendrils of vines. Over time, vine decoration gradually spread until it surrounded the text on all four margins; it also was further embellished with touches of colour or burnished with gold leaf. Sometimes, the artist added little stylised flowers, or painted people, animals and birds disporting themselves among the branches of the vine (1). The grape vine certainly provided an appropriate framework for devotional texts. As well as decorating the borders, it also had symbolic meaning, representing the communion wine and the sacrificial blood of Christ. It even lent its name to the type of ornamental foliage design found in books with the word *vignette*, and to its practitioners with *vignetteur*.

But vines were not the only popular leaf decoration: they were interspersed with a variety of other plants. The most common was ivy, which was thought to have protective properties, and acanthus, with its irrepressible tendency to point and swirl in all directions, making it an irresistible pattern for designs. During the fifteenth century, acanthus succeeded in replacing vines as the dominant leaf in manuscript

*2. Border decorations of acanthus scrolls, gilded vignettes and a speedwell from the Bedford Hours.*
*French, c.1423. Add. MS 18850, f.65.*

borders (2). Some plant symbolism derived from biblical sources, but a great deal more was inherited from the classical world, both in the form of pagan legend (vines and ivy were both sacred to Bacchus) and from the works of the founding fathers of European botany Theophrastus (372–257 BC), Dioscorides (c. AD 40–90) and the elder Pliny (AD 23–79), whose writings remained a source of reference for many centuries.

The borders that surround the text and miniatures of a medieval manuscript could easily be mistaken as being purely decorative, while the miniatures quite obviously relate to the text. However, in fourteenth-century Italy, the plants depicted in manuscript borders served more than a decorative purpose and their symbolic and practical uses began to necessitate a move towards realism. One example, is a *Treatise on Vices*, written by a member of the Cocharelli family of Genoa for the instruction of his children. In this manuscript, the fragments of the text that remain are encircled by the wonders of nature. One sea-blue page displays the creatures of the deep, another serves as a bestiary of exotic animals, but most are adorned with gourds, olives, vines and flowers weighed down by gigantic crickets or caterpillars, spiders and scorpions (3). The skill with which these creepy crawlies have been observed renders them delightful. Yet, they also have a threatening aspect. In the context of this manuscript they could be seen as predators or miniature demons set to prey on the plants in the margins just as the sinful tempt and deceive the unwary. As Cocharelli used it to teach his children, it was necessary that these creatures and plants were convincingly real. This inclusive approach to biology

3. Small red flowers, possibly roses, with large insect predators, from a Treatise on Vices. Italian, late fourteenth century. Add. MS 28841, f.7v.

and morality is not incongruous; commentaries on the religious symbolism of plants were common in medieval sermons and discourse, as it was considered that even the smallest plant or insect reflected the wonder of God's creation and his divine purpose.

Another example is the herbal, in which depictions of plants were of practical importance. These quasi-scientific handbooks of medical prescriptions, tried and tested by many generations, included descriptions of plants accompanied by illustrations, but these were inherited from classical prototypes and centuries of copying had rendered them lifeless and often unrecognisable. The new impetus towards realism in fourteenth-century Italy inspired the illustrators of herbals. This movement started in the medical schools of Salerno and owed much to Arabic influence.

An early example, which shows the first signs of increased realism in the depiction of plants, is a copy of the text known as the *Circa instans*. Produced around 1300 in southern Italy this manuscript contains a remarkable sequence of illustrations of the plants described in the text. Here, although they are still rendered as if pressed flat onto the page like herbarium specimens, the details of real plants have been freshly observed for the first time in centuries. The artist has certainly captured the delicacy of jasmine and the airy quality of love-in-a-mist as surely as the vulgarity of the dragon arum (4); three illustrations grouped together as artemisias are perfectly recognisable as mugwort, tansy and wormwood. On the other hand, the trees look disconcertingly fragile; a pine tree with its needles and cones and the fruiting plum tree next to it both have the air of tiny seedlings. Sometimes the variation of style is obvious in a single page; one contains a white bryony that must have been spread out before the artist's eye. It twines from its roots at the bottom right of the page, all

4. *Dragon arum illustrated in the Circa instans. Italian, c.1300. Egerton MS 747, f.93v.*

5. *White bryony, sorrel and shepherd's purse illustrated in the* Circa instans. *Italian, c.1300. Egerton MS 747, f.16v.*

round both sides of the text, displaying its berries and tightly twisted tendrils, but at the top of the same page, above the two columns of words that describe them, huddle a flat and formal sorrel and an entirely schematic shepherd's purse (5). The artist's attempt to produce a synthesis between traditional patterns and live models explains the uneasy discrepancies throughout the manuscript. The *Circa instans* marked an important start but it took another century for the essential, three-dimensional character of plants to penetrate the artist's eye and be conveyed confidently onto the page.

Nevertheless, in Italy, the scene was set to inaugurate the all-important fifteenth century, when the depiction of flowers in manuscripts reached its peak. The impulse to combine realism and decoration, which was to characterise the whole period (the age of Van Eyck's Ghent Altarpiece and Botticelli's *Prima Vera*, and *millefleurs* tapestries such as *The Lady and the Unicorn*) was represented in the opening years of the century by the superb Carrara Herbal. This was an Italian translation of an Arabic text by Serapion the Younger, produced for the ruler of Padua, Francesco Carrara. In 1403 he was deposed by the Venetians, and his herbal remained unfinished, with only about fifty illustrations completed. When the Carrara Herbal was being produced Padua was the seat of a famous university, with a medical faculty as thriving as Salerno had previously been. Thanks to this intellectual background and the lordly patronage of Francesca Carrara, the artist of the Carrara Herbal emerged, and viewed afresh the written columns of a manuscript page, treating the area around them as a challenging space in which to display the plant in question to maximum advantage and with that element of surprise that characterises true art.

Thus, growing vigorously across the centre of certain pages, there are fat, pale asparagus shoots, whiskery heads of barley and feathery chamomile. A mugwort grows up the left side of its page, with the main leaf jutting into the centre between two blocks of script, the roots spreading along the base and the flower spike curving over the top of the text (6). Some plants, like mallows and trifoliums, are more conventionally grouped side by side

*6. Artemisia, also called mugwort, illustrated in the Carrara Herbal. Italian, c.1400. Egerton MS 2020, f.12v.*

above the text that describes them, but many plants of the kitchen garden look as if the fruiting stem had been laid all across the bottom half of the page to swell juicily before one's very eyes; especially the various vines, melons, gourds and beans. For realism, beauty and vigour the illustration of a bryony in the Carrara Herbal

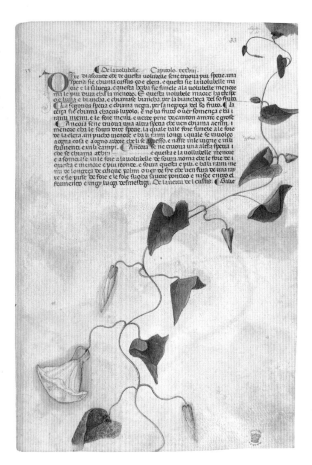

*7. Convolvulus, also called bindweed, illustrated in the Carrara Herbal. Italian, c.1400. Egerton MS 2020, f.33.*

naturally surpasses its predecessor in the *Circa instans*, but most original of all is the stem of convolvulus (7). It spreads diagonally across the space left under the text, with the largest flower at the base pointing downwards, before trailing up the right-hand margin — a complete departure from the convention that stems should be depicted bolt upright (they seldom grow that way).

The British Library possesses another north Italian herbal compiled in this period, showing similar creative impulses and evidently drawn from live plants, although done by clumsier and more conventional hands. Known as the Belluno Herbal, because it was made in that region of the Venetian Alps, it has the endearing and eclectic quality of being compiled as the plants became seasonally available. For instance, a hellebore root and leaf are separated from their green flowers by a hundred pages. Most of the medicinal entries are taken from the classical botanical work of Dioscorides, in the original Latin. There are also comments in Italian, and much of the writing is arranged around the plants like notes around a real specimen, pressed and preserved in a herbarium collection. Thus a handsome martagon lily holds the centre page, with its whorls of leaves and turk's-cap flowers, flanked on one side by its bulb and on the other by its seed-heads; the notes are placed around the flowers where they will fit (8). When the roots of a particular plant are considered its most important part, they are depicted with particular care.

Plant classification in the Belluno Herbal seldom corresponds to any method now in use. On one page hops and bindweed are placed side by side because they are both twining up poles; asparagus and capers appear together presumably

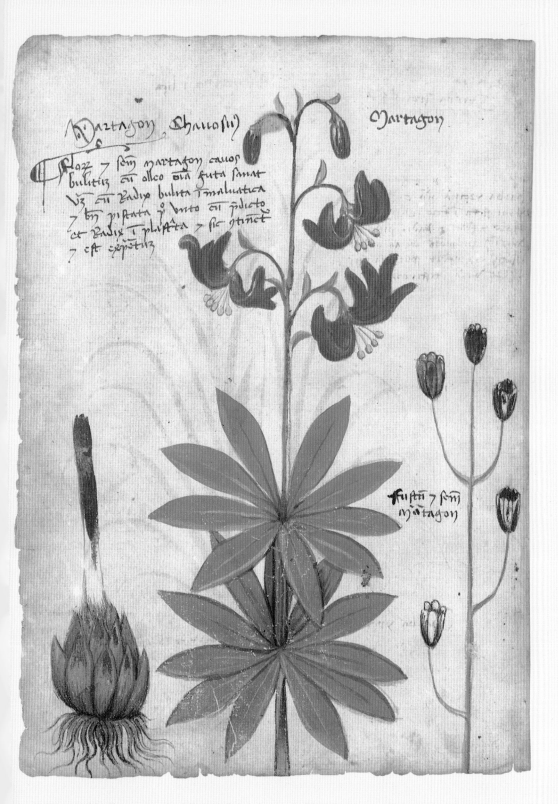

8. Martagon lily illustrated in the Belluno Herbal. Italian, early fifteenth century. *Add. MS 41623, f.66v.*

11

*9. Carline thistle illustrated in the Belluno Herbal. Italian, early fifteenth century. Add. MS 41623, f.97v.*

for culinary reasons. On the other hand bittersweet and physalis are on consecutive pages and do belong to the same plant family. Most unusual of all are the alpine plants local to the region where the herbal was made, edelweiss, gentian (although without flowers) and a carline thistle (9). This is the largest and most dramatic image in the herbal: viewed from above the flower is like a sunburst, with the rays of the petals extending into the green outer rays of the acanthus-like leaves. It is named *oculus bonus*, representing the protective, all-seeing eye of heaven.

Despite these exciting examples, where we are seeing the flowers depicted realistically, most manuscript herbals of the fifteenth century retained their more traditional and lifeless illustrations; and in the wider field of manuscript decoration, as far as Italy was concerned, innovative representations of the natural world occurred only in isolated examples, while most border decoration remained formal and stylised. One of the most astonishing decorative flower studies to survive from these early decades – which seems, however improbably, to be the direct descendant of the Carrara Herbal – was produced much further north, around 1415, by an anonymous Dutch master illustrating prayerbooks. He is named 'The Master of the Morgan

Infancy Cycle' after a manuscript now in the Morgan Library in New York and from its unusual miniatures depicting the childhood of Christ. Similarly, innovative miniatures by this master appear in another prayerbook, now in the British Library, and here the border decorations include real plant forms. The loveliest of these is a pen-work sketch of a pea around the text page opposite the Nativity of Christ (10). The stems curve abundantly round three sides of the border, the flowers are white with flopping petals like folded linen and one flower droops on its stem into the centre of the gilded initial. The splitting peapods are washed with colour, as are the

10. *Pea flowers and pods from the Hours of the Master of the Morgan Infancy Cycle. Dutch, c.1415. Add. MS 50005, f.23.*

slender, twisted leaves, and their forms are made to contrast strongly with the circular peas. Yet all this delight in the patterns to be found in nature occurs only once in all this Master's manuscripts, as if the peas in some particular way celebrated the birth of Christ. Such triumphs of illustration remained few in the Netherlands until later in the century.

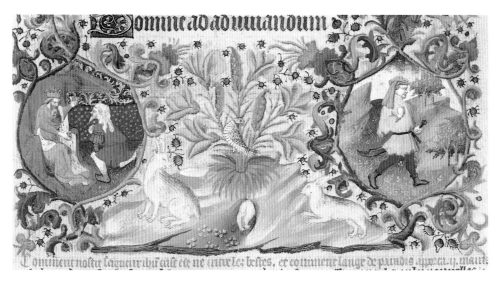

11. Broom flowers and pods, associated with royalty, growing over a rabbit hole surrounded by rabbits and droppings. Bedford Hours. French, c.1423. Add. MS 18850, f.65.

Fifteenth-century prayerbooks often took the form of Books of Hours, so called because they contained the devotions for different hours of the day. These were associated with a sequence of miniatures including the Annunciation at Matins and the Nativity at Prime (both services performed very early in the morning). Other typical elements of Books of Hours included a calendar of saints' days, prayers to particular patron saints, psalms, prayers for the dead and sometimes an extra sequence of Hours to honour the Passion of Christ, all of which could be accompanied by miniatures or border decorations. In France, manuscript border designs became increasingly sumptuous and stately. Among the vine and acanthus scrolls, and the medallions with tiny narrative scenes which were typical of this period, well-known flowers such as violets, daisies, pinks, cornflowers, stocks, strawberries and roses created patterns of colour. The Book of Hours created for the Duke of Bedford is a fine example of the Parisian style, created by a group of associated miniaturists and decorators, centred in little workshops in the narrow streets of the Left Bank, who would exchange the written pages of manuscripts and fill in that part of the design which was their particular expertise. Among those who contributed to the Bedford Hours was an illuminator who enjoyed plants, either displaying them just as they grew, or weaving them into garlands, or introducing a drollery element by placing them above rabbit holes rendered fertile with droppings (11).

There was an additional reason for using plants, since they were emblematic and reinforced the status of the owners. John, Duke of Bedford became Regent of France in 1422, when his brother Henry V, the hero of Agincourt, and Charles VI, the mad king of France, both died, leaving as their joint heir the infant Henry VI. In 1423 Bedford married Anne of Burgundy, creating a powerful dynastic alliance (against which Joan of Arc later rebelled). The Bedford Hours therefore celebrated the union of the Duke and his Duchess, their power, their wealth and their togetherness. There are two portrait miniatures; the Duke is surrounded by golden roots, an emblem previously used by Edward of Woodstock, the Black Prince, who also won famous victories against the French; and the Duchess has a decorative border of yew branches with red berries. Our perception of yew has been tainted by the poisonous reputation of its berries and by the Romantics who considered it funereal. The Duchess of Bedford probably saw it as protective. Yew wood performed a protective function when fashioned into weapons, and yew trees were planted in churchyards and by houses to ward off evil. On another page, where the yew branches of the Duchess are combined with the Duke's rootstock, surrounding their armorial shields and

mottos, the Duchess' berries also suggest the hope of fertility for this dynastic alliance – such emblematic meanings were a vital component of courtly display (12).

Other plants that received prominent treatment in the borders of the Bedford Hours had attributes which explain their inclusion; broom

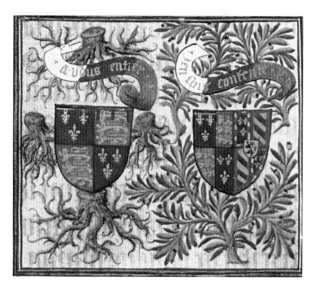

12. The arms of the Duke and Duchess of Bedford with rootstock and yew branches. Bedford Hours. French, c.1423. Add. MS 18850, f.255v.

flowers and pods (11), *planta genista*, have been most associated with the royal Plantagenets, but in fact both French and English kings intermittently adopted broom pods as badges. Similarly the iris, stylised as the *fleur de lys*, was the main emblem of French royalty, which the English appropriated. The legend of how the French king Clovis adopted the iris, because he associated it with a crucial victory, is the subject of a miniature in the Bedford Hours, proving that the significance of an iris was not lost on this lordly couple setting up their court in Paris. Was the garland of red and white roses surrounding a cockerel also significant? (13) The red rose known as *Rosa gallica officinalis* was associated above all with France and the troubadours, but it was also important for medicine and perfume. The link between red roses and the House of Lancaster, to which John of Bedford belonged, dated back to the thirteenth century when Edmund, Duke of Lancaster, brother of Edward I, adopted the red rose as one of his emblems. Later the white rose, *Rosa alba*, was adopted by the House of York; but their rival claims to the English throne were not yet an issue in the 1420s and cannot be relevant in the Bedford Hours. Here the roses could well be intended as another symbol of married union, like red and white pinks, which also appear in the borders of the Bedford Hours and were often used in portraits associated with marriage.

Flowers and leaves, even roots, pods and berries, were a recurring feature on manuscript pages. They could represent every facet of life from medicine to marriage, besides being emblems of power, whether earthly or heavenly. With hindsight their various appearances can be construed as a continuing development leading up to the great flowering of plant decoration in manuscripts in the 1480s.

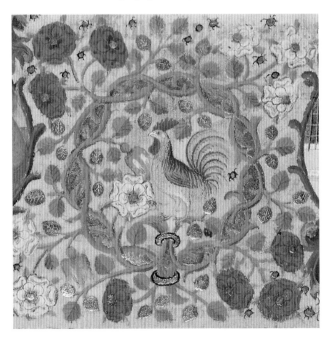

13. *A garland of red and white roses surrounding a cockerel. Bedford Hours. French, c.1423. Add. MS 18850, f.54v.*

# THE GREAT FLOWERING

In the 1470s, there emerged a new manner of depicting flowers in manuscripts. In the southern Netherlands, especially the Flemish towns of Ghent and Bruges, flowers were now being drawn to seem as if they had been plucked from their stems and then scattered over the golden or coloured borders that surrounded the miniatures and texts. Artists used *trompe l'oeil* shadows, to make it look as if real flowers had landed on the page. Insects appear to have alighted, with wings outspread, overlapping the flowers and sometimes even the frames and edges of the text, enhancing the three-dimensional illusion. Artistic practice, like botany, had its precedents in classical tradition. According to the elder Pliny, grapes painted by the Greek painter Zeuxis had been so realistic, so rounded and so shaded, that birds flew down to the painting to peck at them. Awareness of this legend would have added to the resonance of this new style of depicting insect-luring flowers that now appeared in Flemish manuscripts (14).

These decorative borders strewn with flowers were mainly associated with Books of Hours and Breviaries which recorded religious festivals, saints' days and masses for the dead. On such occasions flowers were scattered, before an image of the Virgin, or a saint, either as it was carried in procession or inside the church. In springtime, violets were especially associated with the Annunciation to the Virgin because this was celebrated in March, nine months before Christmas. Pentecost in May was a festival of summer flowers, often culminating in the release of a profusion of

14. Irises with insects and a snail from the Hastings Hours. Flemish, c.1480–83. Add. MS 54782, f.132.

15. Christ washing the disciples' feet. The border shows lilies, white roses (Rosa alba) and speedwells. Hastings Hours. Flemish, c.1480–83. Add. MS 54782, f. 265v.

petals from on high to represent the descent of the Holy Spirit on the disciples. And flowers were certainly used to celebrate marriage or to honour the dead – as they still are now – but it was usual actually to throw them. Tributes of flowers, scattered or in vases, can be seen before the Virgin and Child in many a fifteenth-century painting, and it was equally prevalent for painters to set religious scenes in gardens, which were full of symbolic flowers and reminiscent of paradise or Eden.

The question is therefore not why flowers should be an appropriate decoration for prayerbooks, but whether some flowers were more appropriate than others. Did their increasing variety express the wonder of God's creation or the dawning of a more scientific curiosity and keener awareness of the artist's own creative potential? And did the teasing humour, so evident when manuscript borders were decorated with drollery figures and monsters, also affect the flowers? Consider the lilies. On the one hand they were the archetypal flower symbolising the white purity and golden blessedness of the Virgin. On the other hand, like roses, they had been cultivated in the Mediterranean world long before her time and had many other associations. Lilies were spread throughout Europe by the Romans, not primarily for their beauty or purity but for the relief of the legions, as a cure for corns and bunions. Was it for this latter reason that they made an appearance around the miniature of Christ washing the disciples' feet? (15) Similarly, one might ask whether, when butterflies settled on rosebuds alongside a miniature of the Annunciation, they deliberately mimic the Angel Gabriel landing beside the Virgin and the Holy Spirit descending upon her? (16)

Such puzzles occur repeatedly in the pages of the Hastings Hours, so named after its first known owner William, Lord Hastings, Chamberlain and boon companion of Edward IV (17). Hastings embodied many of the links established between England and the Burgundian state during the fifteenth century, when the dukes of Burgundy held sway from the vineyards around Dijon to the rich sea-trading ports of the Netherlands and were renowned for their magnificence and patronage of the arts. It was Hastings who undertook the negotiations preceding the marriage of Edward IV's sister Margaret of York to Charles the Bold, the last duke, in 1468. He continued to exchange visits with the ambassador Louis of Gruuthuse, a leading bibliophile at the Burgundian court (whose house in Bruges can still be visited) and he helped Edward to lay the foundations of the collection

16. The Annunciation, the border includes wild roses, pinks, daisies, stocks, speedwells, borage, forget-me-nots and sorrel. Hastings Hours. Flemish, c.1480–83. Add. MS 54782, f.73v.

of Royal manuscripts (now in the British Library), as well as encouraging Caxton's new printing venture in Westminster. Hastings' own Book of Hours was the second he had made in the wonderfully innovative style then being developed in the Flemish towns, under the patronage of the Burgundian court. It must have been completed and delivered before 1483 because that year, when Edward IV died, Hastings remained loyal to the succession of Edward's young sons, the Princes in the Tower, and was executed by Richard III.

The flowers used to decorate the Hastings Hours show a fascination with variety, definitely a sign that the artist was also a plantsman. For instance, as well as

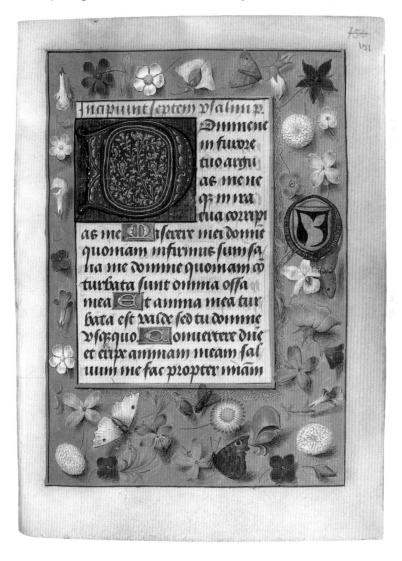

*17. The border design includes the Hastings coat of arms surrounded by stocks, roses, heartsease, rosemary, aconite, daisies, borage, speedwell, campanula, pea and strawberry flowers. Hastings Hours. Flemish, c. 1480–83. Add. MS 54782, f. 151.*

white lilies there is the more unusual orange lily. Daisies come double and single, red, pink or white (or white tipped with red), campions and stocks are red or white, violets are purple or white. Heartsease, the little wild viola from which pansies derived, appear in several combinations of blue, purple, pink, yellow and white (18); in pea flowers the central petals are sometimes pink; the black smudges inside a

*18. Heartsease, speedwell and strawberry flowers. Hastings Hours. Flemish, c.1480–83. Add. MS 54782, f. 52.*

broad bean flower are lovingly observed. As for roses, all the varieties cultivated in the fifteenth century are represented. One dramatic ruby border is entirely devoted to *Rosa gallica* (ancestor of all red roses). This rose is seen from every possible angle, the vibrant petals richly contrasting with the bright emerald leaves and golden stamens (19). When a double white rose appears in a border it is *Rosa alba*, itself an ancient hybrid

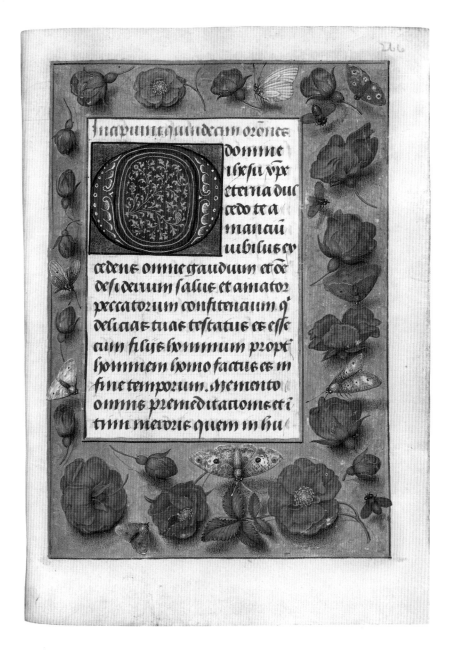

19. *Red roses* (Rosa gallica officinalis). *Hastings Hours. Flemish, c.1480–83. Add. MS 54782, f.266.*

between the wild rose and the damask rose (although the latter seems not to have been cultivated in northern Europe until the sixteenth century and does not appear in art). The extreme delicacy of wild roses, both pink and white, rests softly on these pages.

However freshly observed, none of these flowers was new to cultivation, except perhaps certain types of pinks. (Before the fifteenth century only the bright, basic pink of the wild species seems to have been known.) The Hastings Hours offers important confirmation that red, white and salmon pink varieties existed by the time of its production (20). Judging by their size and prevalence in these borders pinks were of equal symbolic importance to the lilies, roses and irises. Their generic name, dianthus, is Greek and means God's flower. To this was added a piquant Christian symbolism because wild pinks look like cloves or nails, and therefore recalled the nails with which Christ was crucified. By similar association any four-petalled, cruciform flower (like stocks or speedwell) symbolised the crucifix itself; and the sword-like leaves of an iris stood for the spear that pierced Christ's side or (since this was a time when the adoration of Mary almost displaced her own son) the sword-like agony that entered Mary's own heart.

All well-known plants had multiple meanings and a Christian context often superseded an even earlier association or use. Daisy-type flowers were dedicated to Athene and Artemis, the great virgin and moon goddesses of the Greek and Roman world, before they became associated with Mary. Heartsease was a source of love spells (the French called it *pensées*, 'thoughts') before its blended colours made it a flower representing the Trinity. Strawberries could just as well suggest sensual delights as the sweetness of Christian purity, or drops of Christ's redeeming blood. The iris, bearing the purple colour of royalty, or the blue of the sky, conveyed heavenly messages to other faiths besides Christianity.

20. St Margaret with a border decoration of salmon-pink pinks with daisies, borage and speedwells. Hastings Hours. Flemish, c.1480–83. Add. MS 54782, f.62v.

Irises provide two of the most stunning borders in the Hastings Hours. In one (14), all shades of blue glow against the golden background as their petals flop and spread, lying randomly as if they had just fallen on the page, enticing flies, dragonflies, butterflies and an encroaching snail. In the other (21), the dark, heavy iris flowers alternate with sprays of pink cranesbill. Their small, symmetrical flowers, frilly leaves and dainty 'cranesbill' seed pods form a most original contrast with the stately iris. Everything about this border is special: its artistic flair and the scientifically accurate observation of plant characteristics (including the golden beards of the iris and the almost unsightly sheath beneath each flower). One other border (22) shows a flower stem complete with a seed pod, a greater celandine. It appears with a wide variety of flowers including primrose, periwinkle and orange hawkweed. Like the cranesbill, these would all have been wayside weeds.

*21. A border decoration capturing the contrasts between irises and cranesbills. Hastings Hours. Flemish, c.1480–83. Add. MS 54782, f.65.*

The word 'weed' is perhaps unfair. These plants were wild and plentiful but also beautiful and useful, and there may have been special reasons for their selection. In the context of a prayerbook the clue might be a symbolic or linguistic use, and it could refer to anything from a healing property to a forgotten proverb. For instance, several of these flowers had links with birds, which, through their gift of flight, represented the spirit. Cranesbill, because of the shape of the seedcases, was first named in Greek geranium from *geranos*, a crane. Hawkweed, because hawks were believed to eat the plant to strengthen their keen eyesight, was named hieracium from the Greek *hierax*, a hawk. Celandine derived from the Greek *chelidon*, a swallow, because it was supposed to flower and fade with the arrival and departure of the swallow. And here too there was a link with eyesight since the orange juice exuding from the celandine's stem was used (by people and allegedly by swallows) to cure clouding of the vision (don't try this at home, it is a powerful irritant).

22. *A border of wayside weeds, including ground ivy, daisy, periwinkle, speedwell, violets, greater celandine (including the seedpod), primrose and hawkweed. Hastings Hours. Flemish, c.1480–83. Add. MS 54782, f.49.*

The wings of the soul and a clearer spiritual vision make good starting points for constructing symbolic links. Periwinkles may also take on symbolic meaning: their Latin name *vinca* means binding, which alluded to their strong runners and suggested binding the soul to God.

The illuminators' interest both in the plants themselves and in their significance is also relevant to the debate among art historians about methods of manuscript production. Traditionally the credit for these innovative borders has been given to the miniaturist, and in a manuscript like the Hastings Hours the harmony between the central image and the border surrounding it makes this a natural assumption. But detailed studies, especially of manuscripts that have remained unfinished, and of guild regulations, prove that by the fifteenth century a manuscript was produced by many people and in many stages. Pages passed from the scribe to decorators who specialised in different skills: gilding, scrolling, ornamental capitals, drollery figures or flowers. The miniaturist might even be working in a different town, sending what were known as 'detached miniatures' for inclusion in a manuscript which must therefore have been coordinated by some other person. Regardless of who organised the production of the Hastings Hours, it is evident that the most interesting flower borders were created around text, not miniature, pages. This observation suggests that flower studies were not the work of the miniaturist.

There are other differences between the flowers that surround the text and those that surround the miniatures. The latter were more often treated as elements in a recurring pattern of red, white and blue, with little flowers forming squares and triangles around the larger ones (23). The dominant flowers were usually red, either roses, dianthus or lychnis. The whites included peas, daisies, strawberry flowers, campions or sorrels. The blue flowers, especially jewel-like in their brilliance, were nearly always speedwells, sometimes borage or forget-me-not. (By contrast, on the text pages, the blue flowers also included flax, campanulas, periwinkles, bittersweet and cornflowers.) But the very limitations in the variety of flowers used in the miniature borders created an extraordinary harmony. Their carefully chosen colours echoed those used in the miniatures for garments and landscapes (16, 20 and 23). The patterns of large and small flowers, and the diagonal bands of colour they created made another geometry within the geometry of the margin itself, all of which was arguably more pleasing for framing a picture than the greater botanical and stylistic variety of the text borders. In terms of artistic awareness it was a step towards the purist principles that govern abstract art, and it certainly proves that the potential of flowers was being explored by artists in many ways.

23. The Flight into Egypt, the border includes pinks, wild roses, pea flowers, speedwells, strawberry flowers and sorrel, arranged to form a pattern which is characteristic of this manuscript. Hastings Hours. Flemish, c.1480–83. Add. MS 54782, f.131v.

This experimentation, both artistic and botanical, varies from one manuscript to another, rendering each unique and raising fresh questions about how manuscripts were produced and the links that existed between their creators. The Huth Hours, for example, has no emblem to identify its original owner. Its leather binding is identical to that of another Book of Hours, which was produced in Ghent, and its finest miniatures are by the artist Simon Marmion, who lived some distance away in Valenciennes and died in 1489. The border designs are in the Ghent–Bruges style and a few have the distinctive red, white and blue flower patterns, but in this complex manuscript there are many other types of border decoration. For a start, gold is not the only background colour for the flowers; there are greens, blues and greys. More borders are devoted to one type of flower: violets, heartsease, speedwells, pinks or

24. St Catherine surrounded by white flowers including roses, pinks, daisies, violets, peas, deadnettle, campion, stitchwort. Huth Hours. Flemish, c.1480–85. Add. MS 38126, f.142v.

daisies; or to one colour of flower, especially white (24). Sometimes, white borders seem to have a particular association with purity, as in the case of the virgin Saint Catherine, or with a spiritual event such as Pentecost, but this is not always the case, suggesting that any flower could be used either to convey a message or as a thing of beauty in its own right.

Where the flowers are used to create patterns of colour, there is a preference for soft blue and pink harmonies, which is where the cranesbills reappear. They featured just once in the Hastings Hours, but in the Huth Hours (and in other manuscripts linked with the miniatures of Simon Marmion) they occur often, as does another little pink flower, the centaury (25). Indeed, there is a greater variety of flowers in the Huth Hours, more instances of plants depicted complete with leaves and

25. *The Crucifixion with a border of speedwell, cranesbill and centaury. Huth Hours. Flemish, c.1480–85. Add. MS 38126, f.26v.*

seedcases, and the finest flower studies again appear on text pages, not around the major miniatures. It therefore seems possible that the decorators who specialised in flowers were not mere assistants to a miniaturist, but artists and guild members in their own right, possibly even the organisers who commissioned the scribes' and miniaturists' work.

 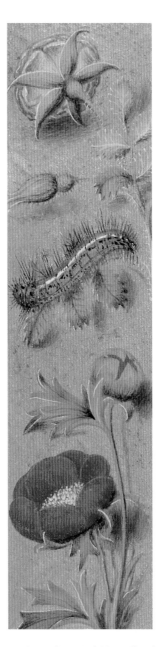 

26. *Lavender. Huth Hours. Flemish,* c.1480–85. *Add.* MS 38126, f.27.

27. *Peony and rose. Huth Hours. Flemish,* c.1480–85. *Add.* MS 38126, f.131v.

28. *Redcurrant. Huth Hours. Flemish,* c.1480–85. *Add.* MS 38126, f.78v.

The flowers cared nothing for such conundrums. In the manuscript borders the flowers evoke the sights and scents of the herb garden: a bee on a spike of lavender (26), curative plants like betony, peony (27) and feverfew, cowslips used for making wine, the gleam of little red fruits like strawberries and redcurrants (28). One humorous border even shows gardening in action, with a woman pushing a wheelbarrow of archaic design containing an enormous red carnation grown in a basket, and a man alongside with another carnation over his shoulder (29). Obviously these flowers are prize specimens, kept under cover during inclement weather and placed in a focal point when in full bloom. Their size suggests they are more important than the people tending them. All of which suggests that these were fashionable flowers, collected, bred and displayed for their variable features.

Whereas, the drollery border in the Huth Hours confirms that flowers could feature in a joke flowers in other borders strike a more sombre note. In the Passion sequence, where there is a small miniature of the Entombment of Christ, an aquilegia grows up the margin (30). This was one of the major symbolic flowers and another that was associated with birds. The likeness of the petals to fluttering wings, and the spurs above the petals to their curving necks and heads, linked aquilegias to Christ's spirit in the form of an eagle (*aquila*) or the Holy Spirit in the form of a dove (*columba*), hence the alternative name columbine. At the same time, purple-blue flowers (not only aquilegias but also violets, violas and irises) bore a colour which was used in mourning, and in places where the prevalent language was French, as in the Burgundian court, the common name for

29. *David Praying, with a drollery border of pinks in a wheelbarrow.* Huth Hours. Flemish. *c.*1480–85. *Add. MS 38126, f.110.*

30. The Entombment of Christ, surrounded by aquilegia, iris and heartsease. Huth Hours. Flemish, c.1480–85. Add. MS 38126, f.29v.

aquilegias was *ancholie*, which was treated as an abbreviation for *melancholie*. Despite the weight of its significance, and the skill needed to capture its complicated petals, this is another exuberant plant, well observed from life. Its developing seedcases are included and there are white flowers alongside the purple as another reminder that colour variation was noted and appreciated.

As in the Hastings Hours, equal attention is lavished on plants whether the symbolism is apparent or not, including wayside plants like bluebells, vetch (31), adonis, bladder campion, centaury, scarlet pimpernel, harebells and mallow. Of these, centaury and mallow were certainly medicinal and adonis had a resurrection symbolism derived from its link with the dead lover of Venus. Rampant weeds like

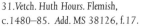

31. *Vetch. Huth Hours. Flemish,*
*c.1480–85. Add. MS 38126, f.17.*

32. *Thistle. Huth Hours. Flemish,*
*c.1480–83. Add. MS 38126, f.198*

corncockle, cornflower, bindweed and thistles (32) feature in some of the most exquisite flower studies of the Huth Hours, created in the half-margins of subsidiary text pages, which is also where the best beetles and hairiest caterpillars are to be found. As in the earlier margins of the Italian *Treatise on Vices*, the insects crawling over the plants may represent an allegory of salvation and sin.

The diversity of its borders is one reason why the Huth Hours has generally been ascribed to a later date than the Hastings Hours. But in the Huth Hours these features are still imbued with a sense of innovation and wonder, which very quickly faded into repetition during the later 1480s. After this crucial decade no new flowers entered the repertoire of the Ghent–Bruges illuminators, while other border designs, including complex architectural frameworks representing church interiors, gained increasing popularity. There was also a proliferation of other motifs such as the bells, badges and shells of pilgrims, or rosaries and cryptograms, or the instruments of Christ's Passion. This proliferation perhaps suggests that the flowers were also regarded as devotional accessories.

By the end of the century, when the Burgundian state was subsumed into the Habsburg Empire and Flemish manuscripts were being produced for the royal ladies of Spain – Isabella of Castile and her daughter Joanna the Mad – luxury prevailed, and flower decorations, although no less magnificent, were far less original. Or sometimes too original, because when daffodils and pinks turn blue it undermines the sense that artistic and scientific integrity were developing side by side. Isabella of Castile, by her marriage to Ferdinand of Aragon and victory over the Moorish armies, unified the kingdoms of Spain, expelled the Jews, imposed rigorous Catholicism which the Inquisition made legendary, and laid the foundations of the Spanish empire in the New World by patronising Columbus. Isabella's Breviary contains coats of arms and an inscription celebrating the marriage of two of her children into the Habsburg dynasty in 1497, an event which almost initiated a united European empire. The Breviary reflects this grandeur, although it also has the uncoordinated look of a manuscript assembled under pressure by a great many different hands. Being designed for the use of priests rather than laity a breviary is fuller than a Book of Hours. In the Isabella Breviary, the Psalms are embellished with a whole series of scenes from the life of David. Of particular interest is David singing with the temple choir, in which each chorister is holding a red rose or a white lily, thus demonstrating how these important sacred flowers might be used on ceremonial occasions (33).

Within the borders there are certain flowers that artists started to use sometime after the Huth and Hastings Hours were produced. Appearing very occasionally, as befits an unusual flower, was the martagon lily (34). It has dark spots on its dusky-pink petals, which curve back and earn it the name Turk's cap. This is a European flower, but not widespread, being choosy about its habitat. Probably it was newly introduced as a garden flower, and perhaps the fiendish problems of painting its recessive petals also deterred artists. Pinks, on the other hand, for as long as they remained single, had a satisfying simplicity and by this time the maiden pink had been added to the repertoire. It is smaller than other pinks, a deep cerise colour, and

33. David and the Temple Choir. The flowers include lily, rose, pea, periwinkle, aquilegia, stocks, campion, heartsease.
*Isabella Breviary. Flemish, 1497. Add. MS 18851, f.146v.*

34. *Martagon lily. Book of Hours. Flemish,*
*c.1500. Add. MS 35313, f.76v.*

has the darker markings at the centre of the flower known as pheasant's-eye. Occasionally in Isabella's Breviary the colour harmonies of the earlier manuscripts are recaptured; in one sumptuous border a dark red background is used to display blue flowers, although they are of varying authenticity. It is possible for a pea flower to develop a blue centre, but the blue lily is confusing, unless it had a meaning that is now lost (35).

Isabella's daughter Joanna the Mad (older sister of Catherine of Aragon), who married into the Habsburg dynasty in 1497, possessed a Book of Hours as small and exquisite as her mother's was large and uncoordinated. The miniature and matching text borders are mainly architectural while the subsidiary text borders contain little drolleries and emblems. Flowers are therefore no longer a dominant motif, but one or two are intriguing, marigolds, for instance, and poppies. If one were to judge their prevalence by a statistical analysis of manuscript borders they would seem as rare as martagon lilies, whereas on the contrary they grew everywhere and were also valued medicinally – perhaps they were simply too bright a colour to fit into the harmonies of manuscript borders. In her Book of Hours the favourite flower of Joanna the Mad was a thistle. It appears often among the drolleries in little sprays or with a golden ring, and has a family background. The Book of Hours of her parents-in-law, Maximilian the Habsburg Emperor and Mary, Duchess of Burgundy, was in production in 1482 when Mary was killed in a riding accident. The manuscript was completed with a proliferation of thistles and the initials MM tied with love knots. According to a family tradition these letters represented not only the names of the tragic couple but the motto *mort et malheur*. The deeply troubled Joanna presumably embraced this tale, and the thistles were added to her own Book of Hours as a symbol of tribulation.

35. *The flowers in the border include iris, rose, pea, aquilegia and a blue lily. Isabella Breviary.*
*Flemish, 1497. Add. MS 18851, f.173.*

Ant Dixit dns. Psalmus

O Nit do
minº
domino
meo sc=
de a dex
tris me
is
Donec ponam inimi=
cos tuos: scabellü pedü tuor

Irgam virtutis tue
emittet dns er syon: dna
rem in medio inimicor mor
Tecum principium in
die virtutis tue in splendo
ribus sanctorum: er vtero i
te luciferum genui te
Iuravit dominus z
non penitebit eum tu es
sacerdos ineternum secu

There is a further Book of Hours in the British Library, known simply as Add. MS 35313 (its British Library shelfmark), which represents a final flowering of the Ghent–Bruges border style. It bears no evidence of ownership except an unidentified coat of arms in the miniature preceeding the Prayers for the Dead. Probably datable to around 1500, it is contemporary with the books of Isabella of Castile and Joanna the Mad. One interesting feature is the drollery of the wheelbarrow with pinks which appeared in the Huth Hours, here featuring a new type of pink (36). In Add. MS 35313 many plants familiar from earlier manuscripts (roses, peas, heartsease and aquilegias) jostle alongside those that always remained unusual (broad beans, mallow, clover, opium poppies, harebells, larkspur and monkshood). There are also flowers that did not appear in manuscript borders until the late 1480s when La Flora was created, including martagon lilies and little white lily flowers such as leucojum and lily-of-the-valley; also a profusion of maiden pinks, including two borders with nothing else but their maroon, twinkly-eyed flowers falling at all angles. Whereas the herb family known as labiates is represented in the Huth and Hastings Hours only by lavender, rosemary and ground ivy, betony, woundwort and hemp nettle are included in later manuscripts such as Add. MS 35313. The hemp nettle (36) has striking purple and yellow markings on its petals, which are sight lines for bees; while a woundwort flower has tiny intricate patterns not often noticed by the human eye. The way these are portrayed proves how closely the manuscript illuminators sometimes worked from nature.

Incapuit lpte plalm
omme ne in furoze tuo

36. *David Praying, with a drollery border of pinks in a wheelbarrow. Above the pinks is a hempnettle. Book of Hours. Flemish, c.1500. Add. MS 35313, f.135.*

# THE FIRST FRENCH FLORILEGIUM

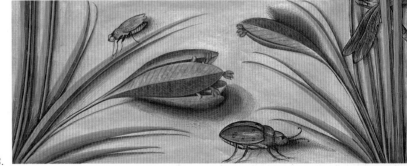

The most famous work of the French illuminator Jean Bourdichon is the Hours of Anne of Brittany, a large and sumptuous volume with fifty miniatures of religious subjects and twelve calendar pages each surrounded with scenes of seasonal occupations, while every text page, of which there are over 350, has a floral border. These are not quite in the Flemish style, although they have golden backgrounds and cast shadows. There is something Italianate and sculptural in the execution, and the flowers seem almost to be set in niches; certainly they are no longer arranged on decorative leaf scrolls, or scattered. This marks an important transition from the earlier adornment of devotional manuscripts – and indeed from herbals, where the illustrations accompany a text on the usefulness of plants – towards the design of a florilegium which celebrates a collection of plants gathered and recorded for their own intrinsic interest or beauty.

Anne of Brittany paid Bourdichon for the completed work in 1508: 'For us he has richly and sumptuously illustrated and decorated a large Book of Hours on which he has spent much time'. By then Anne had been Queen of France for seventeen years, consort first to Charles VIII (the king who owned *La Flora*) then to his successor Louis XII (as heiress to the last independent

*37. Saffron crocus. Bourdichon Hours. French, early sixteenth century. Add. MS 18855, f.78.*

Duke of Brittany an alliance with Anne represented a golden opportunity to enlarge France peacefully). Her payment to Bourdichon was made at Blois, one of the Loire chateaux where the court often resided. Most of Bourdichon's artistic career can be traced around Tours, and one can imagine the plants depicted in his manuscripts growing there.

Anne's ownership of the Hours is confirmed by a portrait miniature that shows her at prayer, while her enjoyment of flowers is depicted in the calendar scene of ladies in a rose garden, where a maid is handing roses to Anne herself. However, the scope of Anne's illuminated florilegium goes far beyond the rose garden or the ornamental flowerbeds: it takes us out into the orchards and the walled kitchen gardens, through the herb gardens where a royal apothecary must have held sway, across the surrounding fields of crops and wild hedgerows and down to the water's edge. The flowers, fruits, stems and twigs that were gathered and painted were also labelled in gold letters, in French above and in Latin beneath, which is generally helpful provided one is not misled by the attempts at classification, which include calling many plants with small black seeds nigella, a name now exclusive to love-in-a-mist. The labelling adds to the sense that this was a florilegium compiled at the behest of the Queen herself, and more than any other feature it distinguishes the Hours of Anne of Brittany from other manuscripts in this style (of which two are in the British Library) where the plants have no labels.

*38. Snowdrop. Bourdichon Hours. French, early sixteenth century. Add. MS 35214, f.17.*

The two British Library manuscripts both contain about a hundred plant illustrations. Since they have no date or mark of ownership it cannot be certain whether they were created before or after Bourdichon's great work for the Queen. One of the Hours in the British Library, known as Add. MS 18855, has an even larger format than the Hours of Anne of Brittany and the presentation of the flowers is very similar. The other, known as Add. MS 35214, is tiny, and here the plants are forced into the two margins along the outer and lower edges of the text pages. They are of necessity elongated, but elegantly so. As usual they have to compete with caterpillars and beetles. The exquisite quality of the artistry of most of the borders raises the speculation that this manuscript may represent an earlier stage in the French adaptation of Ghent–Bruges methods of flower decoration.

Although the roses, irises, lilies, columbines and pinks are as ornamental as might be expected, it is the flowers that are new to the illuminator's repertoire which arouse more excitement, especially when the three manuscripts correspond, confirming their close relationship to one another. To begin at the very start of springtime there is the *primeveize*, as it is called in the Hours of Anne of Brittany. In fact this is the snowdrop making its first appearance in manuscript illumination (38). The distribution of snowdrops through Europe is shrouded in mystery: it is uncertain whether they all originated in Turkey and the Balkans or some are native to other parts. In England snowdrops have a propensity for growing wild in churchyards and the sites of ancient monasteries, and there is a tradition that at Candlemas, in February, they were scattered around the image of the Virgin as an act of purification. This suggests they were widespread before the Reformation when such observances were abolished. An old Flemish name for snowdrops, *lichtmisbloem*, refers to the same medieval festival, but no Ghent–Bruges manuscript includes snowdrops among its scattered flower borders. Only the little white bells of leucojums, or snowflakes, sometimes appear both in the manuscript borders and in fifteenth-century paintings. As late as 1614 when Crispyn de Passe produced his florilegium in the Netherlands, he wrote of snowdrops: 'This plant abounds in Italy, but is not found here except in the gardens of the curious.' Since the first recorded appearance of snowdrops in northern Europe was in the Bourdichon manuscripts, and therefore presumably in the French palace gardens, they serve to launch the Queen's reputation as one of the curious mentioned by de Passe, which in scientific terms meant an avid collector.

plica super nos mīas tuā vt te re
ctore te duce sic transeamus perlo
na temporalia vt non admitta
mus eterna. Per xpm

Scdm
lucam.
Gloria ti
bi domine

Nullotpe.
Missus
est gabriel angelus a deo In cui
tatem galilee cui nomen naza
reth ad virgine desponsatam vi
ro cui nomen erat ioseph de domō
dauid et nomre virginis maria
Et ingressus angelus ad ea dixit.
Aue gra plena dominus tecum.
benedicta tu in mulieribz. Que

39. Daffodil. Bourdichon Hours. French, early sixteenth century. Add. MS 35214, f.15.

40. Adonis anemone. Bourdichon Hours. French, early sixteenth century. Add. MS 35214, f.44.

41. Wallflower. Bourdichon Hours. French, early sixteenth century. Add. MS 35214, f.43.

Many common flowers of springtime – daffodils (39), bluebells, primroses and cowslips, pulmonaria, adonis anemones (40) and forget-me-nots – set the scene, but the yellow wallflower (41) was another novelty in manuscript borders. This, the basic wild species which still prefers growing in the crevices of walls to any other way of life, can be fleetingly traced in medieval garden lists from Moorish Spain, Germany in the time of Frederick Barbarossa and the Paris pleasure garden of Charles V (d.1380) at the Hotel St Pol. But it makes a more lingering appearance in the troubadour legend about a Scottish maiden locked away from her minstrel lover. She threw him a wallflower plucked from the castle battlements, but in attempting to follow her pledge by means of a rope ladder she plunged to her doom. The wallflower therefore became the troubadour symbol of fidelity to a lost love. It was one of the gillyflowers, like pinks and stocks, a name derived from the Italian for cloves, *garofano*, because of their strong sweet scent. The scent also inspired the Latin name *Cheiranthus*, derived from the Greek for a flower to hold in one's hand.

The flowers of later spring which had not previously graced manuscript borders include foxgloves (42) (purple and the more unusual yellow); grape hyacinths, including the oddly tasselled *Muscari comosum* (43); and orchids, named by Bourdichon as a species of satyrion since their sex-enhancing reputation naturally linked them with the legendary activities of satyrs. There are several orchids, which can be tentatively identified as the early purple with its spotted leaves, the pyramid orchid with long spurs behind its flowers, and a bee orchid (44). Almost as arresting in appearance are the euphorbias, including the caper spurge which Bourdichon

42. *Foxgloves. Bourdichon Hours. French, early sixteenth century. Add. MS 18855, f.107.*

43. Tassel hyacinth. Bourdichon Hours. French, early sixteenth century. Add. MS 35214, f.74.

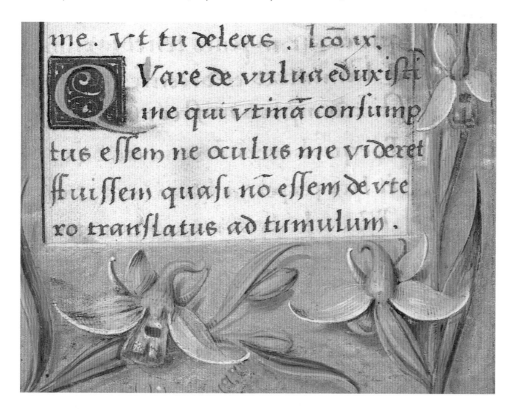

44. Bee orchid. Bourdichon Hours. French, early sixteenth century. Add. MS 35214, f.121.

45. *Cannabis. Bourdichon Hours. French, early sixteenth century. Add. MS 35214, f.64.*

46. *Spindleberry. Bourdichon Hours. French, early sixteenth century. Add. MS 35214, f.84.*

calls *catapucia*, from the Greek for a pill, but not a palatable one since euphorbias are poisonous and act as a very drastic purge. They owe their name to Euphorbus, physician to the north African King Juba (*c*.52 BC – *c*. AD 24), who wrote a treatise on their uses. Although it is doubtful that euphorbias bore much part in the pharmacopoeia of the French court, many other plants that feature in the Hours did have important medicinal qualities. These plants include peonies, yarrow, rosemary, betony, balm, belladonna, plantain, elecampane, feverfew, centaury, comfrey, tansy, mullein, hyssop, opium poppies and cannabis (45).

Not that Bourdichon's plants were grouped either by season, use or habitat, but when describing them it helps to do so. The hedgerows consisted of hawthorns and hazelnuts, brambles, spindleberries (46), wayfaring trees and guelder-rose, entwined with honeysuckle, bryony, hops, bittersweet and old-man's beard. On the banks grew a multitude of wild flowers that live again in the margins of the Hours. So too do the cereal crops of the cultivated fields and the weeds that made them colourful, most still well known, except the dainty purple corncockle, which was dangerous if its poisonous seeds were harvested with the crop, and cow-wheat with its spike of shaggy pink bracts and yellow flowers, which turned bread black. Down by the ponds and streams the plant collector could find yellow iris, marsh marigolds, waterlilies (47), sagittaria, figwort, watercress, and all the surrounding sedges and rushes, and when these arrived on the painted page some were adorned with an appropriate dragonfly.

*Following pages:*
*47. Waterlilies. Bourdichon*
*Hours. French, early*
*sixteenth century. Add. MS*
*35214, f.94v-95.*

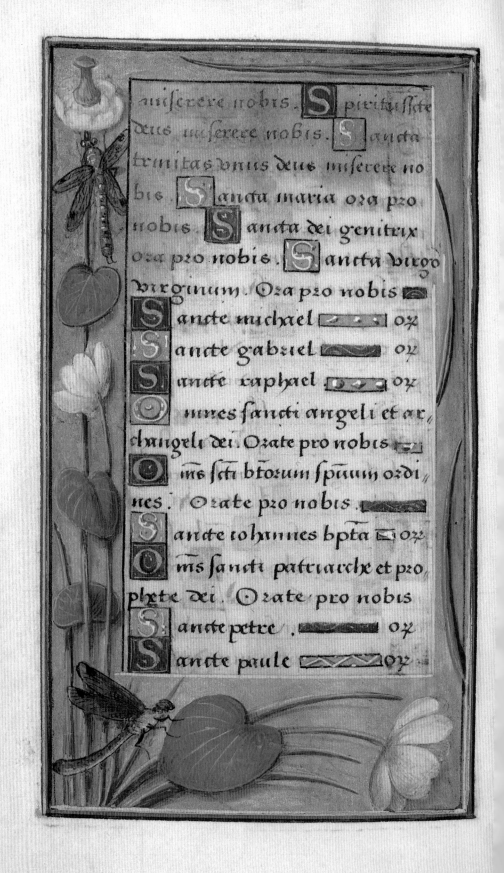

miserere nobis. **S**piritussce
deus miserere nobis. **S**ancta
trinitas vnus deus miserere no
bis. **S**ancta maria ora pro
nobis. **S**ancta dei genitrix
ora pro nobis. **S**ancta virgo
virginum. Ora pro nobis
**S**ancte michael oꝛ
**S**ancte gabriel oꝛ
**S**ancte raphael oꝛ
**O**mnes sancti angeli et ar
changeli dei. Orate pro nobis
**O**mes scti btorum spuum ordi
nes. Orate pro nobis.
**S**ancte iohannes bpta oꝛ
**O**mes sancti patriarche et pro
phete dei. Orate pro nobis
**S**ancte petre. oꝛ
**S**ancte paule oꝛ

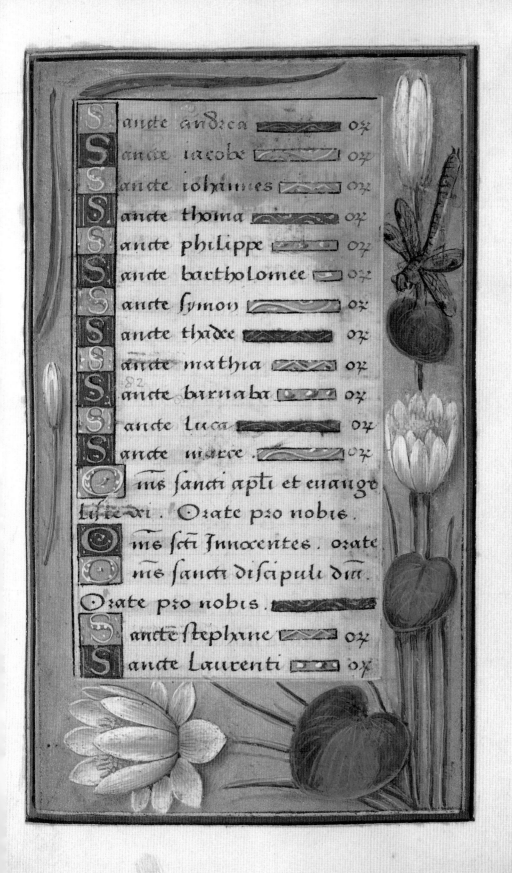

S anete andrea ⸻ oꝛ
S anete iacobe ⸻ oꝛ
S anete iohannes ⸻ oꝛ
S anete thoma ⸻ oꝛ
S anete philippe ⸻ oꝛ
S anete bartholomee ⸻ oꝛ
S anete symon ⸻ oꝛ
S anete thadee ⸻ oꝛ
S anete mathia ⸻ oꝛ
S anete barnaba ⸻ oꝛ
S anete luca ⸻ oꝛ
S anete marce ⸻ oꝛ
O mis sancti apli et euange
liste di . Orate pro nobis .
O mis scti Innocentes . orate
O mis sancti discipuli diu .
Orate pro nobis ⸻
S anete stephane ⸻ oꝛ
S anete Laurenti ⸻ oꝛ

In the days when the range of plants was limited mainly to native species, and their usefulness as food or medicine rendered them vital, the boundaries between wild and cultivated plants were more blurred than they are now. Were the ragged robin (48), lupin, orpine and campanulas hedgerow plants or

48. *Ragged robin. Bourdichon Hours. French, early sixteenth century. Add. MS 35214, f.63.*

inhabitants of the flowerbed, or both? Were sempervivums (49) grown merely on rooftops or were they an object of fascination in a garden trough? Bourdichon, in naming them *barba jovis*, confirms that the filaments growing over certain sempervivums like a venerable white beard were noted and appreciated. Like the

49. *Sempervivums. Bourdichon Hours. French, early sixteenth century. Add. MS 35214, f.47v.*

Ghent–Bruges illuminators Bourdichon bears witness to an increasing fascination with colour variation, offering the first purple iris with contrasting maroon falls, the first double yellow ranunculus, the first candytuft and also the first sweet williams (50). Never before had this type of dianthus been mentioned or illustrated (Bourdichon's are red), and it was not until 1554 that the German botanist Dodoens published the first description (although before that Henry VIII had planted quantities at Hampton Court so it is fair to assume it was then the *dernier cri* as a garden plant).

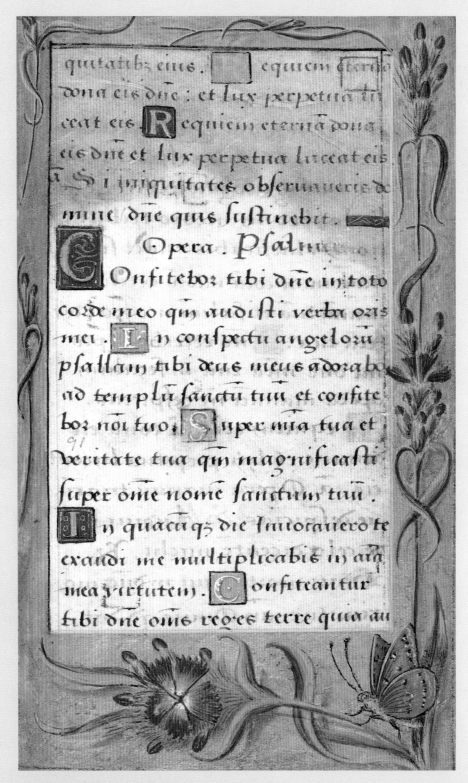

quitatibz eius . [ ] equiem eterna
dona eis dne : et lux perpetua lu
ceat eis [R]equiem eterna dona
eis dne et lux perpetua luceat eis
[S] i iniquitates obseruaueris do
mine dne quis sustinebit . [ ]
[ ] Opera . Psalm
[C]onfitebor tibi dne in toto
corde meo qui audisti verba oris
mei . [I]n conspectu angeloru
psallam tibi deus meus adorabo
ad templu sanctu tuu et confite
bor noi tuo . [S]uper mia tua et
veritate tua qui magnificasti
super oe nome sanctum tuu .
[I]n quacuqz die inuocauero te
exaudi me multiplicabis in aia
mea virtutem . [C]onfiteantur
tibi dne oes reges terre quia au

50. *Sweet williams. Bourdichon Hours. French, early sixteenth century. Add. MS 35214, f.104.*

In Bourdichon's Hours we come full circle. Just as fourteenth-century Italian herbals owed a debt to Arabic plantsmanship, so the more exotic plants depicted in his margins were those first cultivated in the gardens of Islam. These plants include, hollyhocks, where the debt was acknowledged in the French name *rose d'outremer*; physalis (51), whose other name *alkekengi* is Arabic; the yellow dye plants, safflower, like an orange thistle, and the stunning saffron crocus (37) with its precious golden pollen bursting from its skirt of silky petals. Bourdichon also offers the first proof that

51. *Physalis. Bourdichon Hours. French, early sixteenth century. Add. MS 35214, f.53v.*

jasmine (52) had moved into France from Spain (where it was listed in the plantings of Moorish gardens) and Italy (where Boccaccio set the scene for the storytellers of the *Decameron* by adorning the garden arbours with jasmine). Of the Asian plants first featured in Northern Europe by Bourdichon, the most recent introduction was probably the celosia (53), a deep red pompom of flowers, which would have needed Anne of Brittany's newly created hothouse in which to over-winter (alongside her oranges). Celosias remained a rare and tender plant and not until the eighteenth century did painters include them in their flower and fruit still lifes.

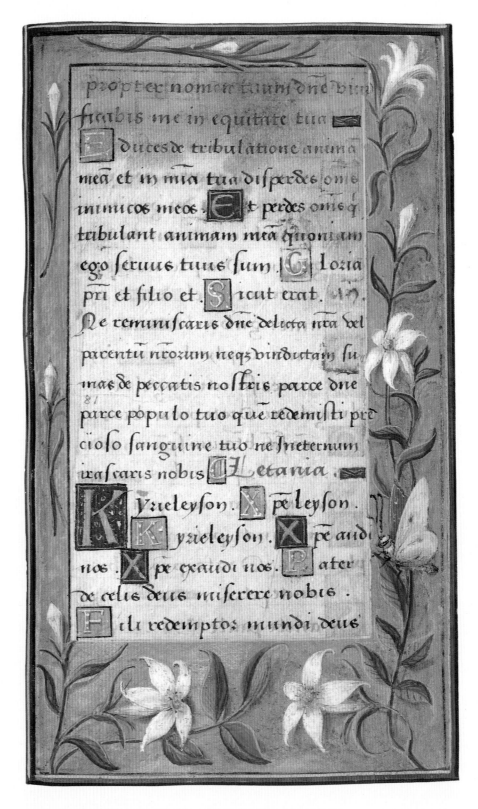

propter nomen tuum dne viui
ficabis me in equitate tua ☙
☐ duces de tribulatione anima
mea et in mia tua disperdes oms
inimicos meos . ☐ t perdes oms q
tribulant animam mea quoniam
ego seruus tuus sum . ☐ loria
pri et filio et . ☐ icut erat . ij .
Ne reminiscaris dne delicta nra vel
parentu nrozum neqz vindictam su
mas de peccatis nostris parce dne
parce populo tuo que redemisti pre
cioso sanguine tuo ne Ineternum
irascaris nobis ☐ Letania . ☙
☐ yrieleyson . ☐ pe leyson .
☐ yrieleyson . ☐ pe audi
nos . ☐ pe exaudi nos . ☐ ater
de celis deus miserere nobis .
☐ ili redemptos mundi deus

52. Jasmine. Bourdichon Hours. French, early sixteenth century. Add. MS 35214, f.94.

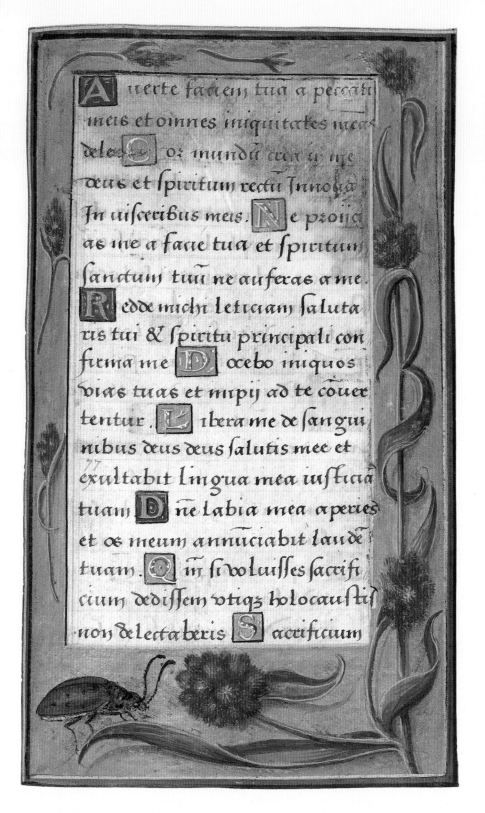

uerte faciem tua a peccati
meis et omnes iniquitates meas
dele○: o: mundu cor in me
deus et spiritum rectu Innoua
In uisceribus meis. Ne proina
as me a facie tua et spiritum
sanctum tuu ne auferas a me.
Redde michi leticiam saluta
ris tui & spiritu principali con
firma me D ocebo iniquos
vias tuas et impij ad te couer
tentur. L ibera me de sangui
nibus deus deus salutis mee et
exultabit lingua mea iusticia
tuam D ne labia mea aperies
et os meum annuciabit laude
tuam. Q in si voluisses sacrifi
cium dedissem vtiqz holocaustis
non delectaberis S acrificium

53. Celosia. Bourdichon Hours. French, early sixteenth century. Add. MS 35214, f.90.

Finally Bourdichon completes his selection of seasonal plants with depictions of holly and mistletoe (54).

Although this plant collection is of undeniable value for the history of botany it was first and foremost a book of prayers. The wonders of nature captured on its pages were therefore intended to enhance the worship of their Creator. Flowers were not an incidental adornment, nor a mere hobby fit for a Queen. Whenever flowers appeared in the borders of medieval manuscripts they also formed a vital part of the biblical message:

*Look how high the heaven is in comparison to the earth...*

*The days of man are but as grass, for he flourisheth as a flower of the field,*

*As soon as the wind goeth over it, it is gone.*

(Psalm 103 vv. 11 & 15–16)

*Opposite:*
*54. Mistletoe.*
*Bourdichon Hours.*
*French, early sixteenth*
*century. Add. MS*
*35214, f.113.*

erubesco dū veneris iudicare
noli me condennare/quia pec
caui nimis in vita mea. ▬
Jn̄ᵒ n̄ᵒ an̄. Jn loco.
Dn̄s regit me et nichil mi
chi deerit in loco pascue ibi
me collocauit. Super aquam
refectionis educauit me animā
mea conuertit Deduxit me
super semitas iusticie propter
nome suū. Nam et si ambu
lauero in medio vinbre mortis
non timebo mala qm tu mecū es
Virga tua et baculus tuus
ipsa me consolata sunt. Para
sti in conspectu meo mensam ad
uersus eos qui tribulant me.
Jmpinguasti in oleo caput
meū et calix meus inebrias qp

# FURTHER READING

**W. Blunt and W.T. Stearn**
*The Art of Botanical Illustration*
(London, 1950; new edition 1994).

**A. Coates**
*Flowers and their Histories*
(London, 1956; repr. 1968).

**M. Collins**
*Medieval Herbals: the Illustrative Traditions*
(London, 2000).

**M. Grieve**
*A Modern Herbal*
(London, 1931; repr. 1976).

**J. Harvey**
*Medieval Gardens*
(London, 1981).

**P. Hobhouse**
*Plants in Garden History*
(London, 1992).

**T. Kren and S. McKendrick**
*Illuminating the Renaissance: the Triumph of
Flemish Manuscript Painting in Europe*
(London, 2003).

**S. McKendrick**
*Flemish Illuminated Manuscripts 1400–1550*
(London, 2003)

# MANUSCRIPTS LIST

**Add. MS 42130**
Luttrell Psalter. English, c.1300.

**Add. MS 28841**
Cocharelli Treatise on Vices.
Italian, late fourteenth century.

**Egerton MS 747**
Circa instans. Italian, c.1300.

**Egerton MS 2020**
Carrara Herbal. Italian, c.1400.

**Add. MS 41623**
Belluno Herbal.
Italian, early fifteenth century.

**Add. MS 50005**
Hours of the Master of the Morgan
Infancy Cycle. Dutch, c.1415.

**Add. MS 18850**
Bedford Hours. French, c.1423.

**Add. MS 54782**
Hastings Hours. Flemish, c.1480–83.

**Add. MS 38126**
Huth Hours. Flemish, c.1480–85.

**Add. MS 18851**
Isabella Breviary. Flemish, 1497.

**Add. MS 18852**
Hours of Joanna the Mad.
Flemish, c.1500.

**Add. MS 35313**
Book of Hours. Flemish, c.1500.

**Add. MS 18855**
Bourdichon Hours.
French, early sixteenth century.

**Add. MS 35214**
Bourdichon Hours.
French, early sixteenth century.

# PLANT LIST

| Common Name | Botanical Name | Common Name | Botanical Name |
|---|---|---|---|
| acanthus | Acanthus spinosus | convolvulus (bindweed) | Calystegia sepium |
| adonis anemone | Adonis annua | corncockle | Agrostemma githago |
| aquilegia (columbine) | Aquilegia vulgaris | cornflower | Centaurea cyanus |
| artemisia (mugwort or wormwood) | Artemisia vulgaris, A. absinthium | cowslip | Primula veris |
| | | cow-wheat | Melampyrum arvense |
| | | cranesbill | Geranium robertianum |
| asparagus | Asparagus officinalis | daffodil | Narcissus pseudo-narcissus |
| balm | Melissa officinalis | | |
| barley | Hordeum vulgare | daisy | Bellis perennis |
| bean | Vigna species | dragon arum | Dracunculus vulgaris |
| broad bean | Vicia faba | edelweiss | Leontopodium alpinum |
| belladonna (deadly nightshade) | Atropa belladonna | | |
| | | elecampane | Inula helenium |
| betony | Stachys officinalis | euphorbia (spurge) | Euphorbia robbiae |
| bittersweet (woody nightshade) | Solanum dulcamara | | |
| | | caper spurge | Euphorbia lathyrus |
| bluebell | Hyacinthoides non-scripta | feverfew | Tanacetum parthenium |
| borage | Borago officinalis | figwort | Scrophularia nodosa |
| bramble (blackberry) | Rubus fruticosus | flax | Linum usitatissimum |
| broom (planta genista) | Cytisus scoparius | forget-me-not | Myosotis species |
| | | foxglove | |
| bryony | Bryonia dioica | purple | Digitalis pupurea |
| buttercup | Ranunculus species | yellow | Digitalis grandiflora |
| campanula | Campanula species | gentian | Gentiana acaulis |
| campion | | gourd | Lagenaria vulgaris |
| bladder | Silene vulgaris | grape hyacinth | Muscari neglectum |
| red | Silene dioica | tassel hyacinth | Muscari comosum |
| white | Silene latifolia | guelder-rose | Viburnum opulus |
| candytuft | Iberis amara | harebell | Campanula rotundifolia |
| cannabis (hemp) | Cannabis sativa | | |
| capers | Capparis spinosa | hawkweed | Hieracium aurantiacum |
| carline thistle | Carlina acaulis | | |
| carnation | Dianthus species | hawthorn | Crataegus monogyna |
| celandine greater | Chelidonium majus | hazelnuts | Corylus avellana |
| celosia | Celosia argentea | heartsease | Viola tricolor |
| centaury | Centaurium erythraea | heather | Calluna vulgaris |
| chamomile | Chamaemelum nobile or anthemi nobilis | hellebore | Helleborus species |
| | | hempnettle | Galeopsis speciosa |
| | | holly | Ilex aquifolium |
| clover (trifolium) | Trifolium species | hollyhocks | Althaea rosea |
| comfrey | Symphytum officinale | | |

| Common Name | Botanical Name | Common Name | Botanical Name |
|---|---|---|---|
| honeysuckle | Lonicera species | poppy | |
| hops | Humulus lupulus | field | Papaver rhoeas |
| hyssop | Hyssopus officinalis | opium | Papaver somniferum |
| iris (fleur de lys) | Iris germanica | primrose | Primula vulgaris |
| yellow | Iris pseudacorus | pulmonaria (lungwort) | Pulmonaria officinalis |
| ivy | Hedera helix | | |
| jasmine | Jasminum officinale | ragged robin | Lychnis flos-cuculi |
| larkspur | Delphinium ajacis or Consolida ambigua | redcurrant | Ribes rubrum |
| | | rose | |
| lavender | Lavendula officinalis | red | Rosa gallica |
| leucojum (snowflake) | Leucojum vernum | white | Rosa alba |
| lily | | wild | Rosa canina |
| madonna | Lilium candidum | rosemary | Rosemarinus officinalis |
| martagon | Lilium martagon | | |
| orange | Lilium bulbiferum | rushes | Juncus species |
| lily of the valley | Convallaria majalis | safflower | Carthamus tinctorius |
| love-in-a-mist | Nigella damascena | saffron crocus | Crocus sativus |
| lupin | Lupinus albus | sagittaria | Sagittaria sagittifolia |
| lychnis | Lychnis coronaria | scarlet pimpernel | Anagallis arvensis |
| mallow | Malva species | sedge | Carex species |
| marigold | Calendula officinalis | sempervivum | Sempervivum tectorum |
| marsh marigold | Caltha palustris | | |
| melon | Cucumis melo | shepherd's purse | Capsella bursa-pastoris |
| mistletoe | Viscum album | snowdrop | Galanthus nivalis |
| monkshood (wolfsbane) | Aconitum napellus | sorrel edible | Rumex acetosa |
| | | wood | Oxalis acetosella |
| mullein | Verbascum thapsus | speedwell | Veronica species |
| old-man's-beard | Clematis vitalba | spindleberry | Euonymus europaeus |
| olive | Olea europaea | stocks | Matthiola incana |
| orchid bee | Ophrys apifera | strawberries | Fragaria vesca |
| early purple | Orchis mascula | sweet williams | Dianthus barbatus |
| pyramid | Anacamptis pyramidalis | tansy | Tanacetum vulgare |
| orpine (stonecrop) | Sedum telephium | thistle | Cirsium species |
| pea | Pisum sativum | vetch | Vicia sativa |
| peony | Paeonia officinalis | vine | Vitis vinifera |
| periwinkle | Vinca major | violet | Viola canina |
| physalis | Physalis alkekengi | wallflower | Cheiranthus cheiri |
| pinks | Dianthus species | watercress | Nasturtium officinale |
| maiden pink | Dianthus deltoides | | |
| plantain | Plantago major and P. lanceolata | waterlily | Nymphaea alba and Nuphar lutea |
| | | wayfaring tree | Viburnum lantana |
| | | woundwort | Stachys sylvatica |
| | | yarrow | Achillea millefolium |
| | | yew | Taxus baccata |

# THE AUTHOR

Celia Fisher wrote her Ph.D. thesis on flowers in the borders of illuminated manuscripts and is the author of *Flowers and Fruit* (National Gallery, 1998) and *Still Life Paintings* (Vadi, 2000), as well as articles in art and gardening journals. She lectures on plants in art and is a consultant on the subject for Kew Gardens and various art galleries.

Front and Back Cover Illustration:    *Detail from a border decoration capturing the contrasts between irises and cranesbills. Hastings Hours. Flemish, c.1480–83. Add. MS 54782, f.65.*

Half-title Page:    *Lavender. Huth Hours. Flemish, c.1480–85. Add. MS 38126, f.27.*

Frontispiece:    *Red roses (Rosa gallica officinalis). Hastings Hours. Flemish, c.1480–83. Add. MS 54782, f.266.*

Title Page:    *Peony. Huth Hours. Flemish, c.1480–85. Add. MS 38126, f.131v.*

Published in North America in 2004 by
University of Toronto Press Incorporated
Toronto and Buffalo
ISBN 0–8020–3796–8

Text © 2004 Celia Fisher
Illustrations © 2004 The British Library Board
First Published by The British Library

National Library of Canada
Cataloguing in Publication
Fisher, Celia
    Flowers in medieval manuscripts / Celia Fisher.
Includes bibliographical references and index.

    1. Flowers in art. 2.Illumination of books and manuscripts,
Medieval–Europe. I.Title.
ND3340.F57 2004     745.6'7'094     C2004-901740-3

Designed and typeset by Crayon Design, Stoke Row, Henley-on-Thames
Printed in Hong Kong by South Sea International Press